# my first Origami BOOK

ARCTURUS

This edition published in 2019 by Arcturus Publishing Limited
26/27 Bickels Yard, 151–153 Bermondsey Street,
London SE1 3HA

Illustrators: Kasia Dudziuk and Amanda Enright
Designer: Duck Egg Blue
Cover designer: Ms Mousepenny
Writers: Belinda Webster and Joe Fullman
Editor: Kait Eaton at Duck Egg Blue

ISBN: 978-1-78950-321-0
CH007022NT
Supplier 33, Date 0719, Print run 9122

Printed in China

# WHAT IS ORIGAMI?

Origami is the craft of paper-folding, invented in Japan hundreds of years ago. The word "origami" means "folded paper" in Japanese.

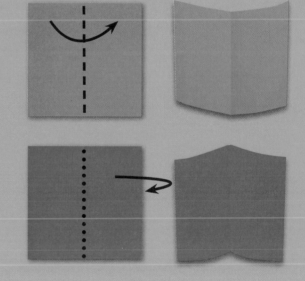

Origami paper is thin but strong, so it can be folded many times.

It is square and is usually white on one side.

You could use ordinary scrap paper instead of origami paper, but make sure it's not too thick.

## BASIC FOLDS

To follow the steps in this book, there are two basic folds you need to learn.

### VALLEY FOLD

To make a valley fold, fold the paper up on itself so that the crease is at the bottom, like a valley. A valley fold will be shown by a dashed line, like this.

### MOUNTAIN FOLD

To make a mountain fold, fold the paper the other way, away from you. You want the crease to point up, like the peak of a mountain. We use a dotted line to show a mountain fold.

## KEY

- - - - - Valley fold

· · · · · · · · Mountain fold

 Step fold (this is a mountain fold and a valley fold next to each other)

↘ Direction to move paper

 PUSH Direction to push (or pull, etc.)

# WINDMILL

Blow on this windmill to watch it spin, or stand it outside and wait for the breeze to make it turn.

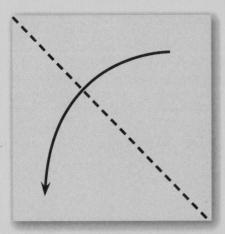

1 Start with the paper white side up, like this. Valley fold it in half, as shown. Unfold.

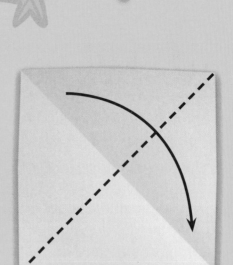

2 Valley fold the paper in half the other way. Unfold.

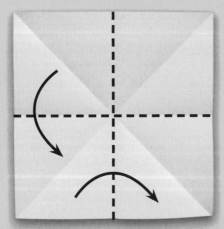

3 Valley fold the paper from top to bottom and unfold it. Then valley fold it from left to right. Unfold.

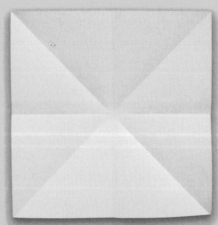

4 Your paper should now look like this.

**5** Valley fold the left and right sides in, so they meet in the middle.

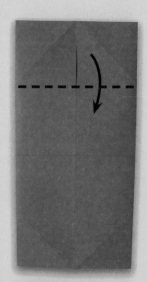

**6** Valley fold the top edge in to the middle. Crease well, then unfold.

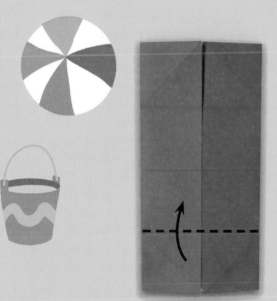

**7** Valley fold the bottom edge in to the middle. Crease well, then unfold.

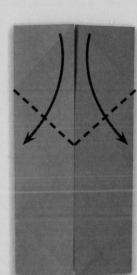

**8** Valley fold the top layer of the top left and right flaps out to the sides, as shown. This will pull the paper behind upward.

**9** Your model should look like this. Pull the top flap down so that it lies flat.

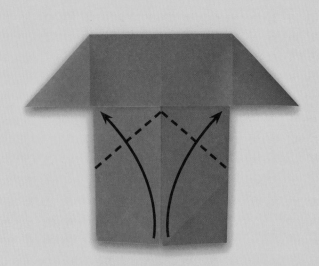

**10** Valley fold the top layer of the bottom left and right flaps out to the sides, as shown.

**11** Your model should look like this. Pull the bottom flap up so that it lies flat.

**12** Valley fold the bottom left flap down.

**13** Valley fold the top right flap up.

**14** Ask an adult to help you use a tack to attach your windmill to a pencil so that you can hold it or stand it up. Blow gently on the windmill to see it turn.

# GHOST

This ghastly ghoul is best made from plain white paper.

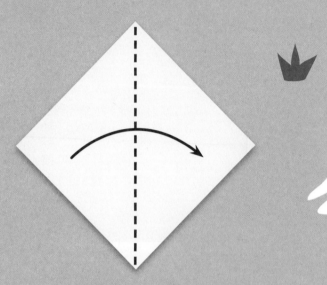

1 Start with the paper like this. Valley fold it in half from left to right. Unfold.

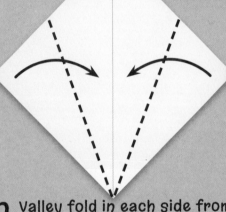

2 Valley fold in each side from the bottom corner so that the edges meet in the middle. This makes a kite shape.

3 Valley fold the flaps on both sides down, as shown. The bottom edges should create a straight, horizontal line.

8

**4** Your paper should now look like this. Turn it over.

**5** Valley fold the small flaps so they wrap around the ghost's body.

**6** Valley fold the sides in, as shown. They should meet on the central crease.

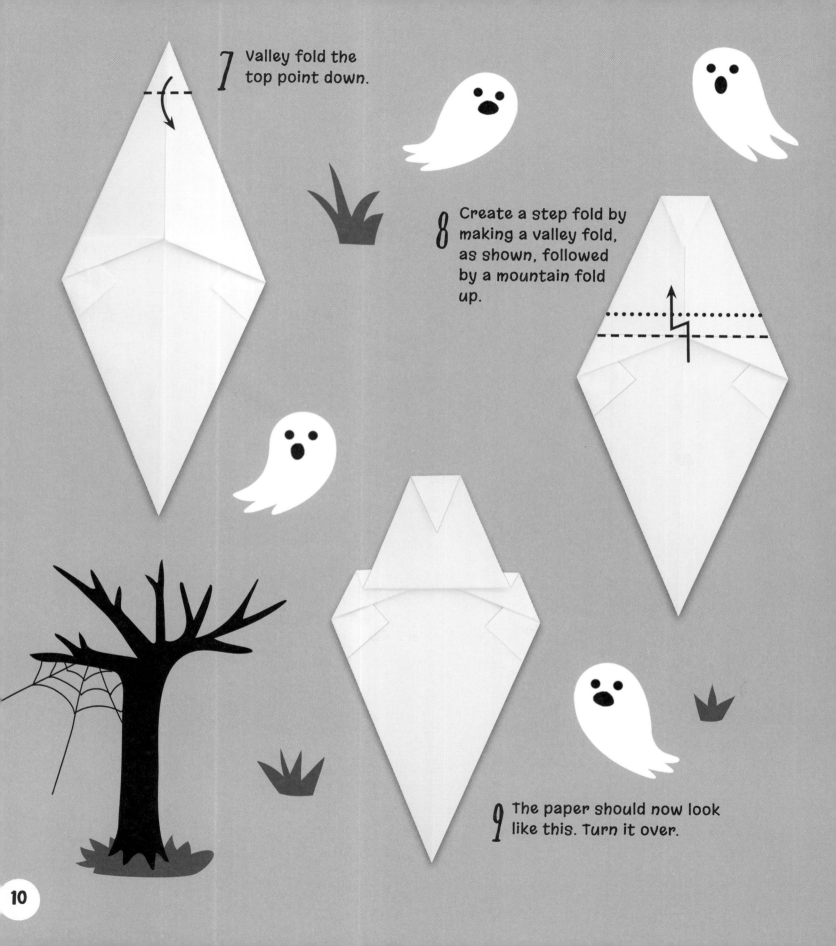

**7** Valley fold the top point down.

**8** Create a step fold by making a valley fold, as shown, followed by a mountain fold up.

**9** The paper should now look like this. Turn it over.

10

**10** Create the ghost's wispy tail by making a valley fold as shown.

**11** Your origami ghost is complete!

GIVE YOUR SPOOKY GHOST EYES AND A WAILING MOUTH.

# ELEPHANT

Elephants are the largest animals on land. Your paper model will be much smaller!

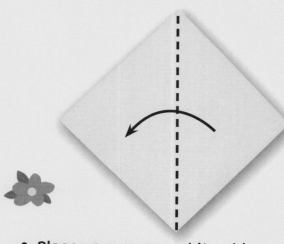

**1** Place your paper white side up, like this. Valley fold it in half from right to left, then unfold.

**2** Valley fold as shown, about a quarter of the way along the bottom left edge.

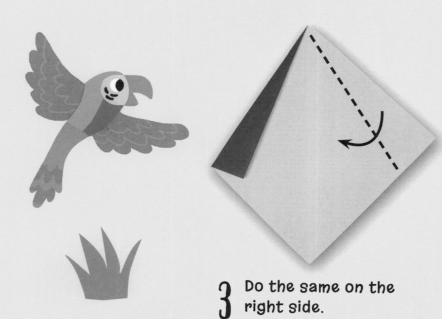

**3** Do the same on the right side.

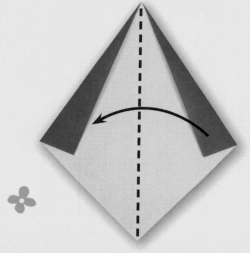

**4** Valley fold the paper in half from right to left.

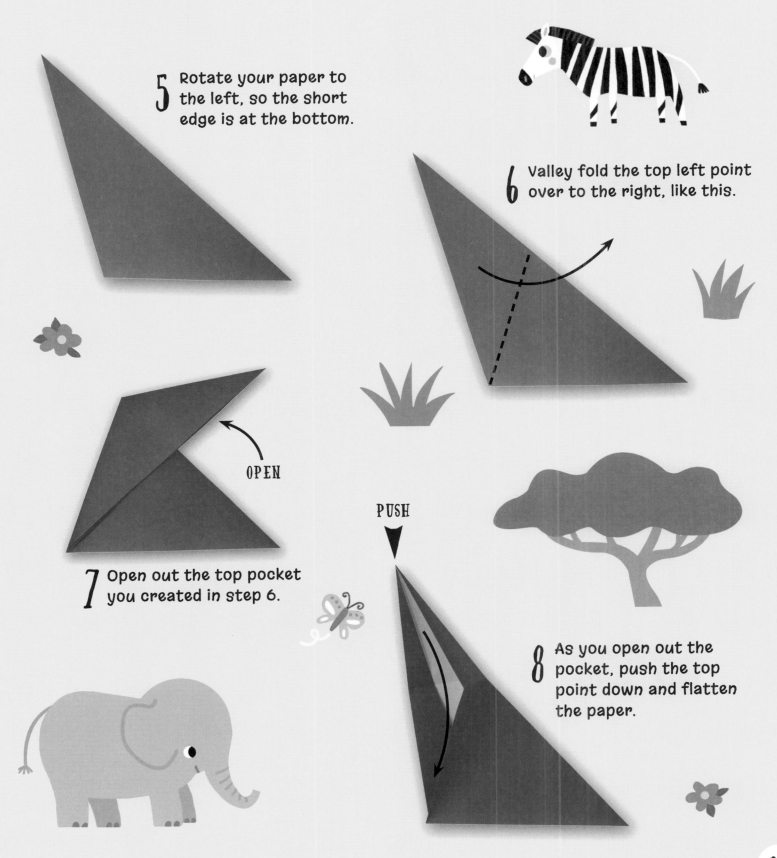

**5** Rotate your paper to the left, so the short edge is at the bottom.

**6** Valley fold the top left point over to the right, like this.

OPEN

**7** Open out the top pocket you created in step 6.

PUSH

**8** As you open out the pocket, push the top point down and flatten the paper.

13

9 Your paper should look like this. On the top piece only, make two small cuts along the solid lines shown. Mountain fold the paper behind on either side.

10 Make one mountain fold, followed by a valley fold, as shown in stage 1 above. Then make another mountain fold, followed by a valley fold, as shown in stage 2. These two step folds will create the elephant's trunk.

11 Your paper should look like this. Flatten the folds.

12 Make a mountain fold, followed by a valley fold, to create a step fold on the left-hand side, as shown. This will be one of the elephant's ears.

**13** Repeat step 12 on the right-hand side, to create the other ear.

**14** To make the elephant's tail, valley fold the right-hand point as shown. Then mountain fold it along the same crease. Unfold so it is flat again.

**15** Create another valley fold, to the right of the fold you just made. Then mountain fold it back along the same crease, as you did in step 14.

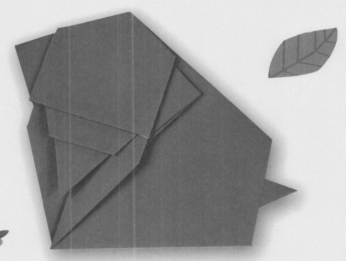

**16** Open out the end of the paper and tuck the tail inside the body along the crease you made in step 14. Flatten. Then fold it out along the crease made in step 15. Flatten. The tail should poke out, as shown.

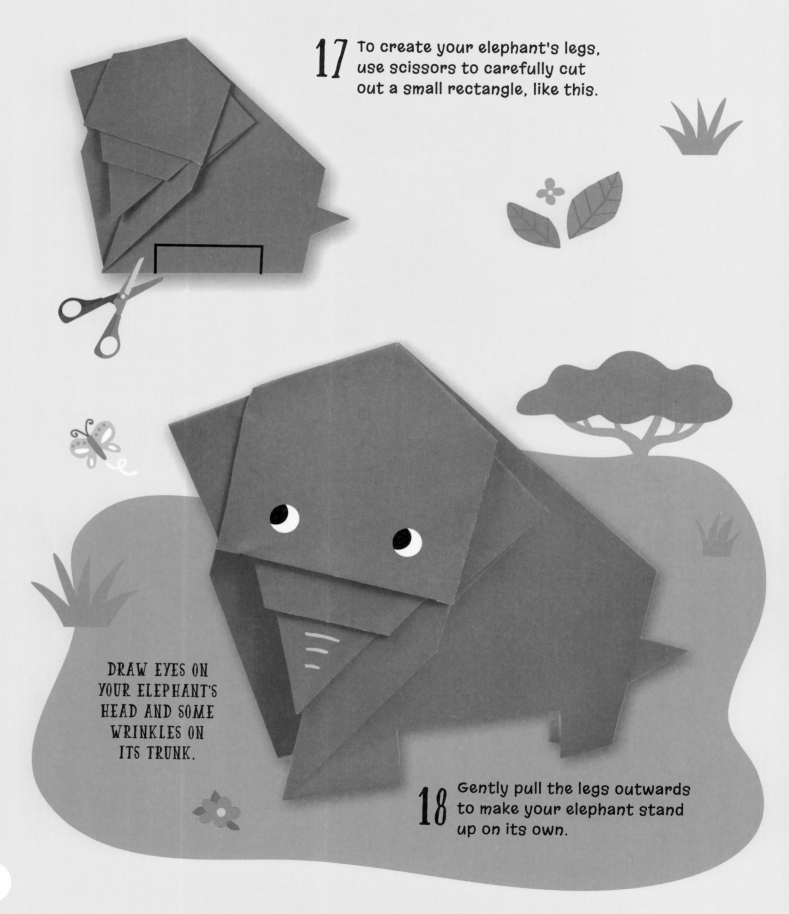

**17** To create your elephant's legs, use scissors to carefully cut out a small rectangle, like this.

DRAW EYES ON YOUR ELEPHANT'S HEAD AND SOME WRINKLES ON ITS TRUNK.

**18** Gently pull the legs outwards to make your elephant stand up on its own.

# PENGUIN

Penguins waddle when they walk. If your origami model wobbles, don't worry— it will look more like the real thing!

**1** Place your paper white side down, like this. Valley fold it in half from left to right, then unfold.

**2** Turn over the paper so that the crease becomes a mountain fold. Valley fold the right corner as shown, about a quarter of the way along the bottom right edge.

**3** Do the same on the other side.

**4** The paper should now look like this.

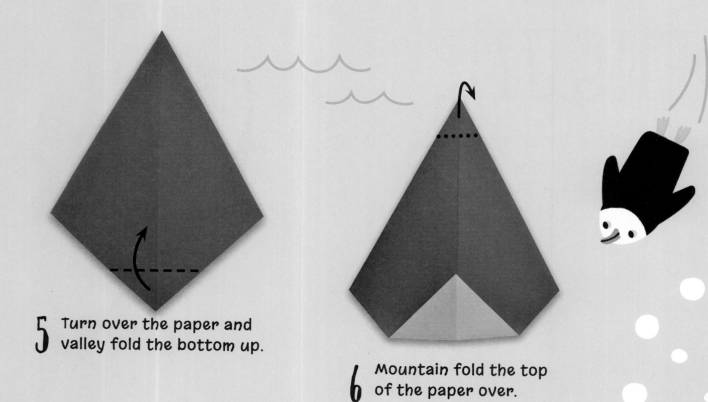

5 Turn over the paper and valley fold the bottom up.

6 Mountain fold the top of the paper over.

7 Valley fold the paper in half from left to right.

8 Valley fold the corner tip. This is the penguin's wing. Do the same on the other side.

PULL

**9** Now pull up the beak. Flatten the paper so the beak points outward.

DRAW SOME CUTE EYES ON YOUR PENGUIN.

**10** Stand up the model. Your origami penguin is complete!

# RABBIT

Make your own sweet little rabbit with super-long ears by following these steps.

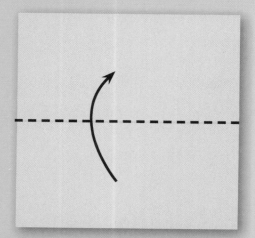

1 Place your paper white side up. Valley fold as shown, then unfold.

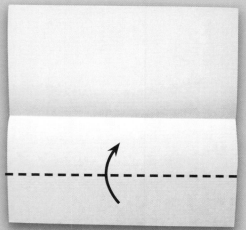

2 Valley fold the bottom section up to meet the middle crease.

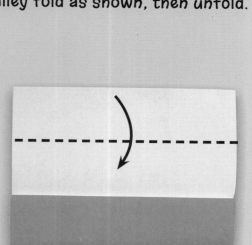

3 Do the same with the top section.

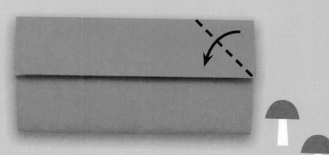

4 Valley fold the right corner down to meet the middle crease.

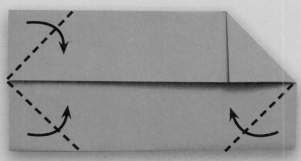

**5** Valley fold the other corners in the same way.

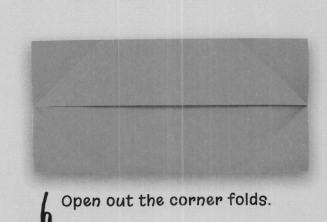

**6** Open out the corner folds.

TUCK IN

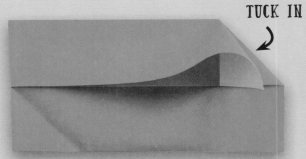

**7** Gently push the top right corner inside to create a flap along the creases, as shown. Flatten.

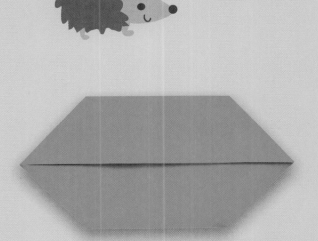

**8** Do the same with the other three corners.

**9** Turn over the paper. Valley fold the top layer of the left point and flatten down.

**10** Do the same with the other side.

**11** Your paper should now look like this.

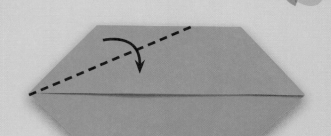

**12** Turn over the paper. Valley fold the top left corner to meet the middle crease, as shown.

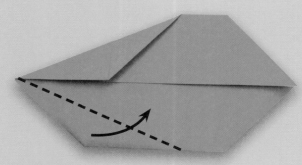

**13** Do the same with the bottom left corner.

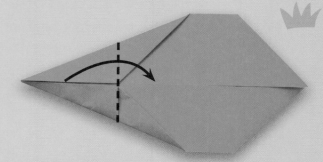

**14** To make the rabbit's ears, valley fold the left point, as shown. The flap underneath pops out to become the rabbit's nose.

**15** Mountain fold the paper in half, along the middle crease.

PULL

**16** Gently pull the ears up.

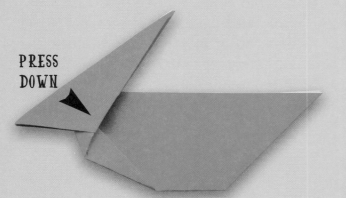

PRESS DOWN

**17** Press the paper as shown to flatten the head in position. Your paper should now look like this.

**18** Valley fold the right point so the diagonal edge runs flat along the bottom of the model. Unfold.

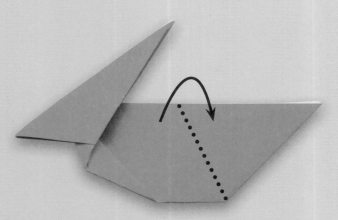

**19** Mountain fold along the same crease, then unfold. Open out the right end and fold the points inward, into the body. Flatten along the creases to make feet.

**20** Valley fold along the line, as shown, then unfold. Mountain fold along the same crease, then unfold. Fold each point inward, into the body. Flatten to create the back of your rabbit.

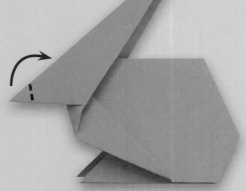

**21** Valley fold along the line, as shown, then unfold. Mountain fold along the same line, then unfold. Tuck the point in along the crease to create a nose.

GIVE YOUR RABBIT EYES, SOME WHISKERS, AND A CUTE NOSE.

**22** Gently puff out the long ears to give them their shape. You now have an origami rabbit!

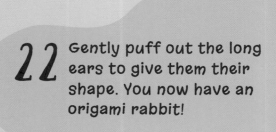